W9-BLB-927

COPYRIGHT © 1994 LANDOLL
World Rights Reserved
LANDOLL
Ashland, Ohio 44805
® Little Landoll Books is a trademark owned by Landoll, Inc.
and is registered with the U.S. Patent and Trademark Office.
No part of this book may be reproduced or copied.
All rights reserved. Manufactured in the U.S.A.

ESTHER

THE

VERY BRAVE QUEEN

by Sunny Griffin

Illustrated by Andra Chase

DID YOU KNOW...
Esther was a beautiful young Jewish girl who lived in Persia with her cousin Mordecai?

DID YOU KNOW...

God had a plan for Esther's life, even though she didn't know it?

DID YOU KNOW...
The king of Persia wanted to marry a beautiful young woman and make her the queen of the kingdom?

DID YOU KNOW...
When King Xerxes
saw Mordecai's cousin
Esther, he fell in love
with her?

DID YOU KNOW...

Esther married King Xerxes and became the new queen?

DID YOU KNOW...
One of the king's helpers, Haman, hated Mordecai because Mordecai would not bow down to him?

DID YOU KNOW...
Haman convinced
King Xerxes to make
a law that Mordecai
and all the Jewish
people should
be killed?

DID YOU KNOW...
King Xerxes did not
know that his
beautiful young
queen was a
Jewish girl?

DID YOU KNOW...
When Mordecai heard the new law, he sent a message to Queen Esther, asking her for help?

DID YOU KNOW...

Even though he had not called for her and she might be punished, Esther bravely went to see the king?

DID YOU KNOW...
Esther invited the king and Haman to a banquet, and there she told the king that Haman wanted to destroy her people?

DID YOU KNOW...

King Xerxes was angry with Haman and told Esther to make a new law to save the Jewish people?

Esther's bravery and trust in God were part of God's plan to keep his people safe in Persia.